CATS, DOGS, and CAT CLUMPS

BOOK 1

ISBN-10: 1497505151
ISBN-13: 978-1497505155

----DEDICATION----

This work is dedicated to all animals that live a life of abuse and all the people and organizations that help them.

----INTRODUCTION----

Every animal life form on this planet has a purpose in the world of Mother Nature, whether in the deepest reaches of the oceans, remotest of jungles, or in our backyards. City Councils everywhere demonstrate their ignorance of this on a daily basis.

Recently, several people in our community decided that they did not like feral cats because they ate birds. Their ignorance was shared and accepted by the Town Council, which in turn passed a clandestine ordinance resulting in the capture and disposing of feral cats.
Mother Nature responded in the usual way. The explosion of every conceivable type of rodent, coyote, rattlesnake, mountain lion, and all types of predators possibly dangerous to humans rushed in to fill the void left by the extermination of feral cats.

Not to mention the destruction of very expensive landscaping all over the community and adjacent communities.

One is reminded of the political process at the local, State, and federal levels.

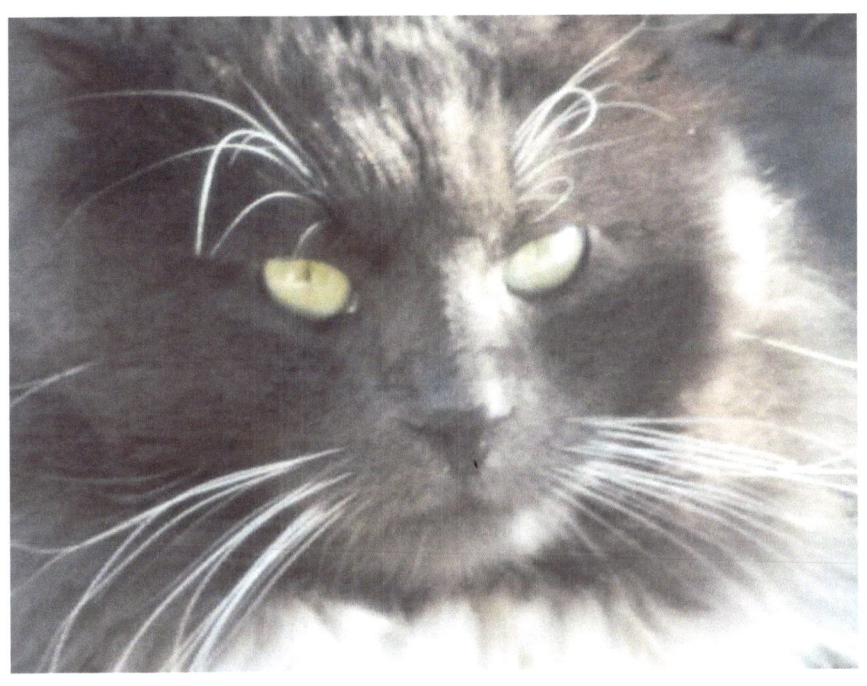

BIG GREY: RULING TOM FERAL: WHEN HE
SHOWS UP, ALL FERALS TAKE TO THE TREES.
BG HAS LITTLE ABILITY IN TREES BUT HE SURE
RULES THE GROUND FLOOR.

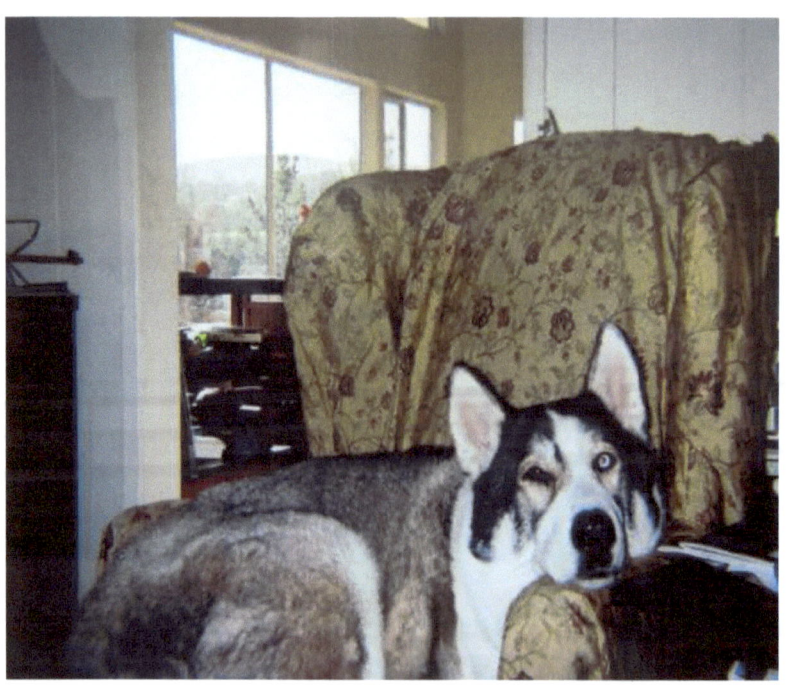

JUST ANOTHER DAY IN PARADISE

Sonny returned to us after being gone for five years.
Wonder where he was? Sonny does act as though
each new day back home is a day in Paradise.

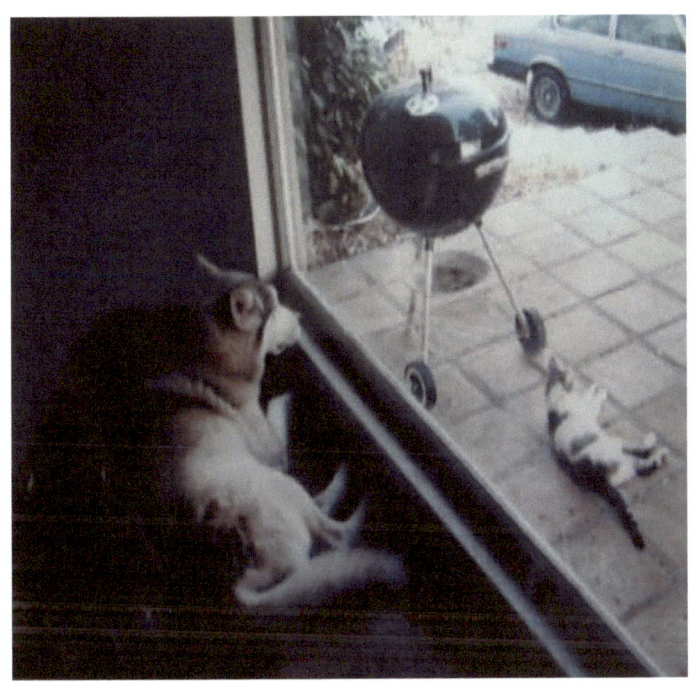

COPY CAT

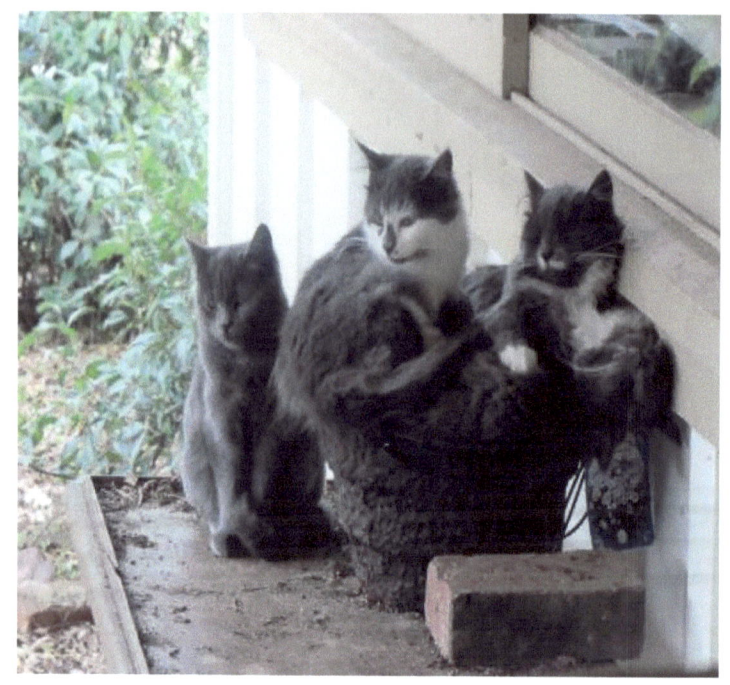

CAT CLUMP IN VARIOUS SLEEP STAGES

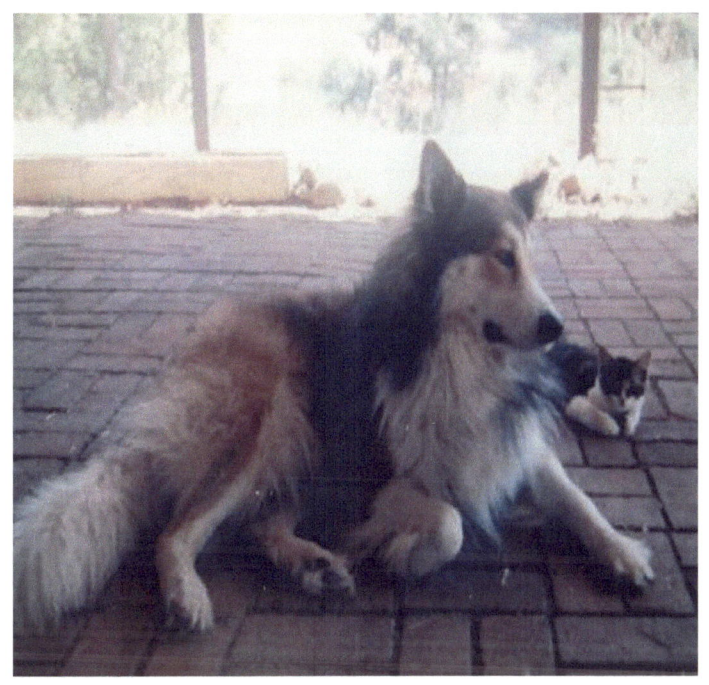

YES DEAR, I REQUESTED A VIEW TABLE

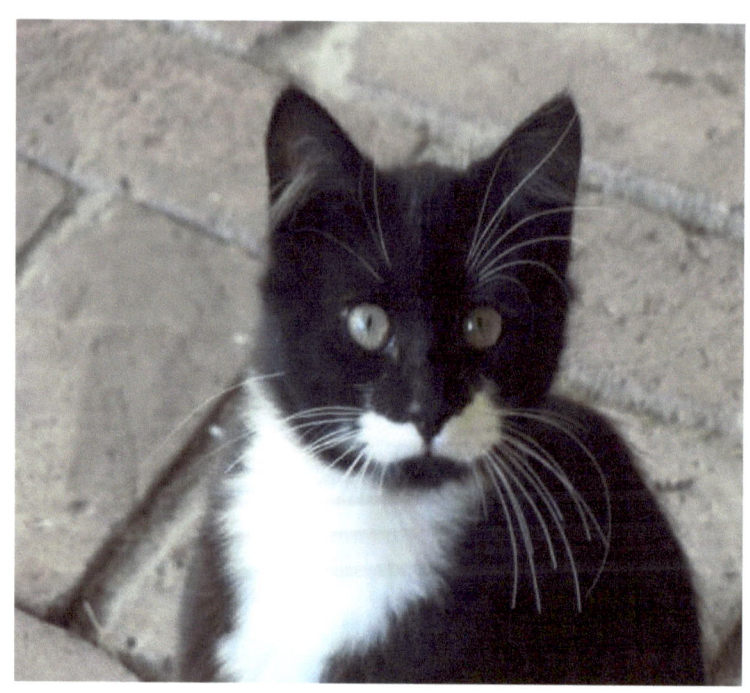

GOT MILK ?

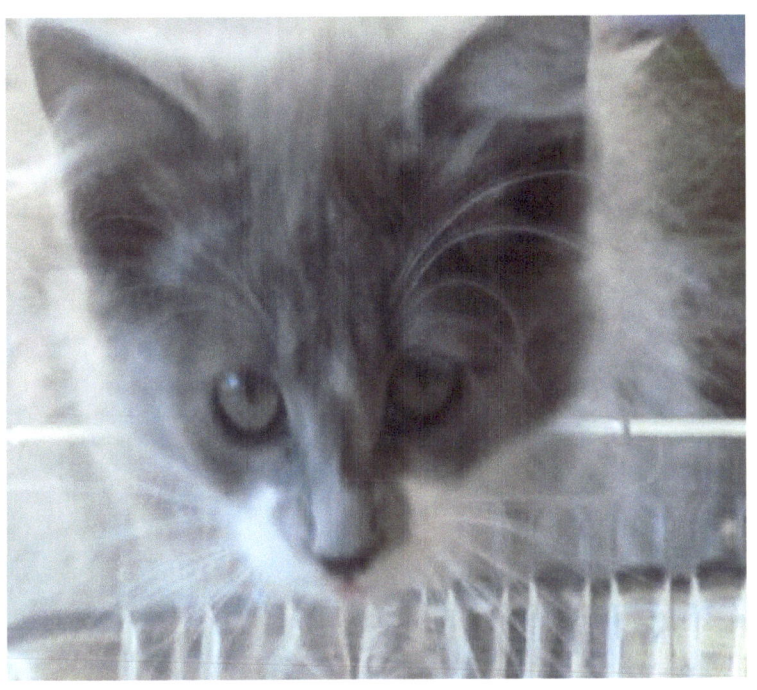

GOT MORE MILK ?

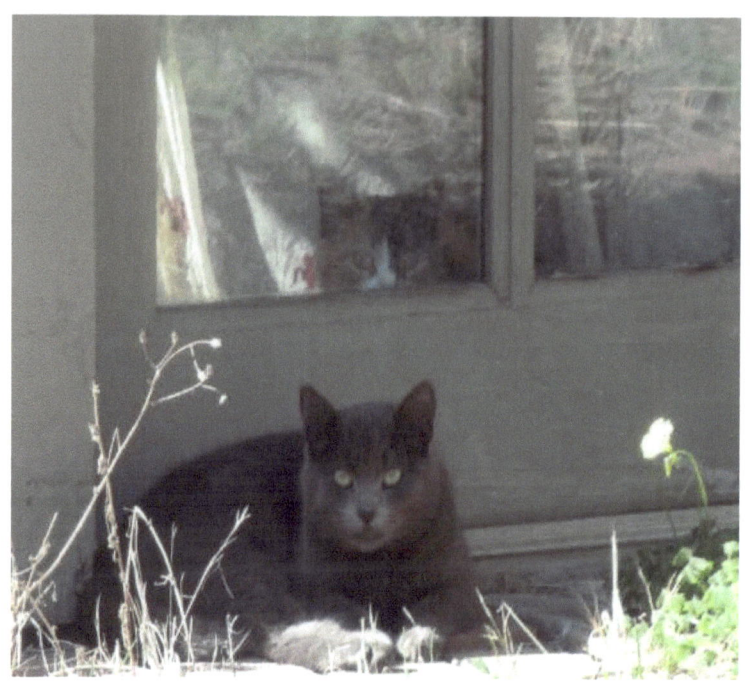

MR. INSIDE AND MR. OUTSIDE

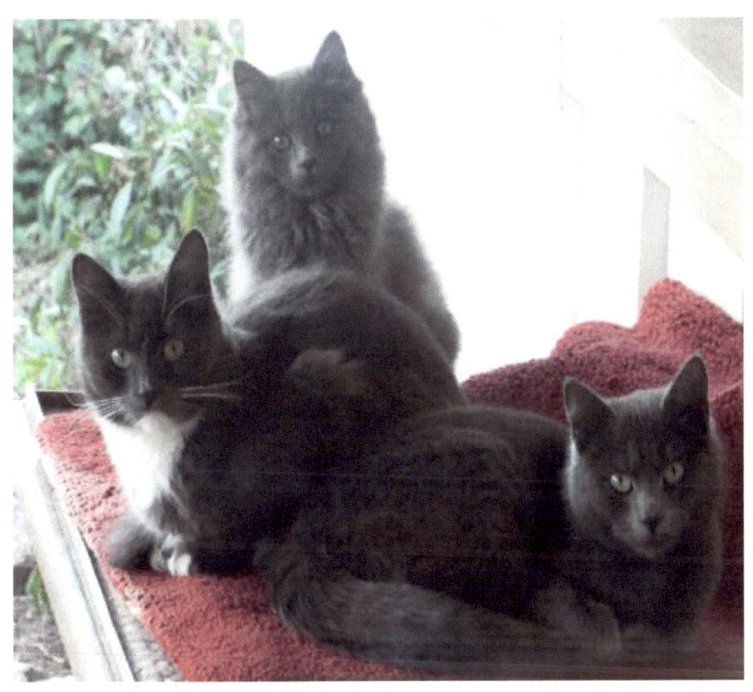

CAT CLUMPING ON THE RED CARPET

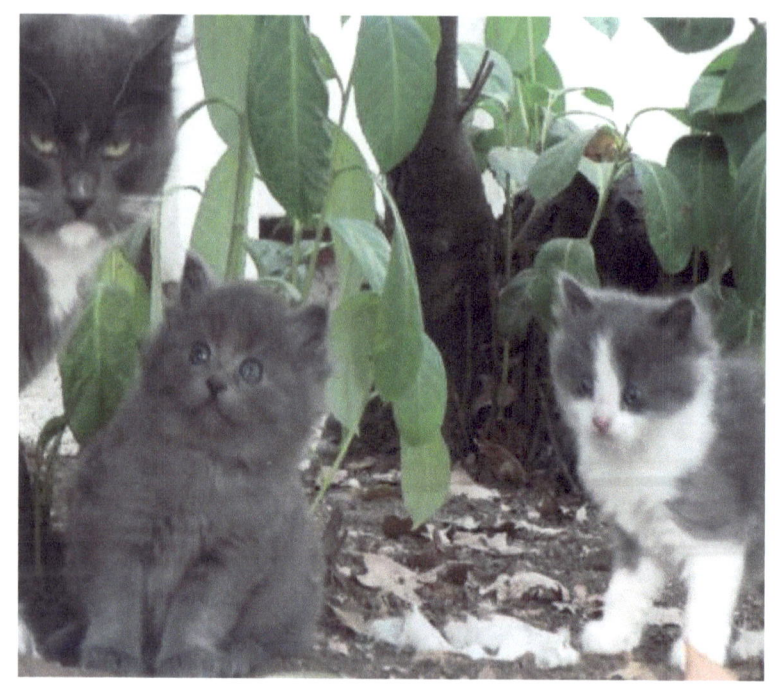

SORRY MOMMY, BUT YOU SAID TO FART OUTSIDE

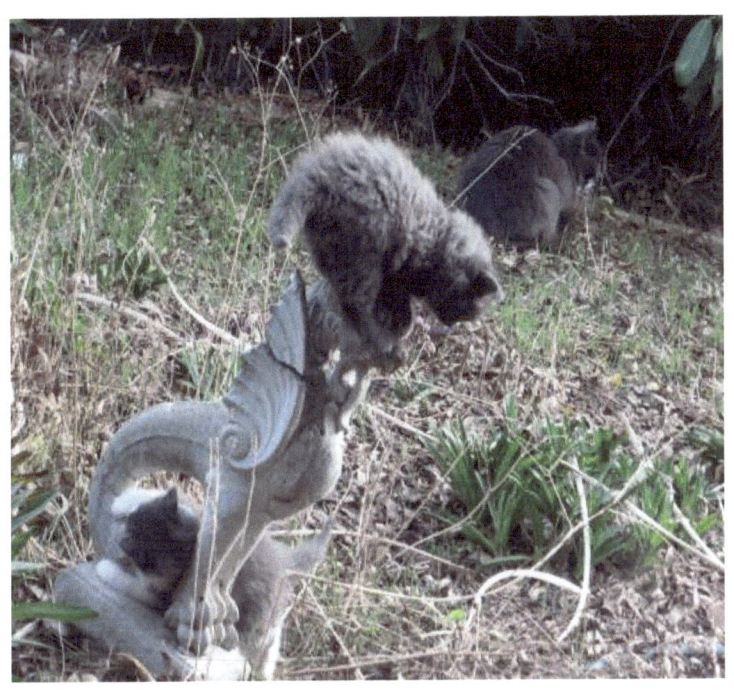

GOING DOWNNNnnn!!!

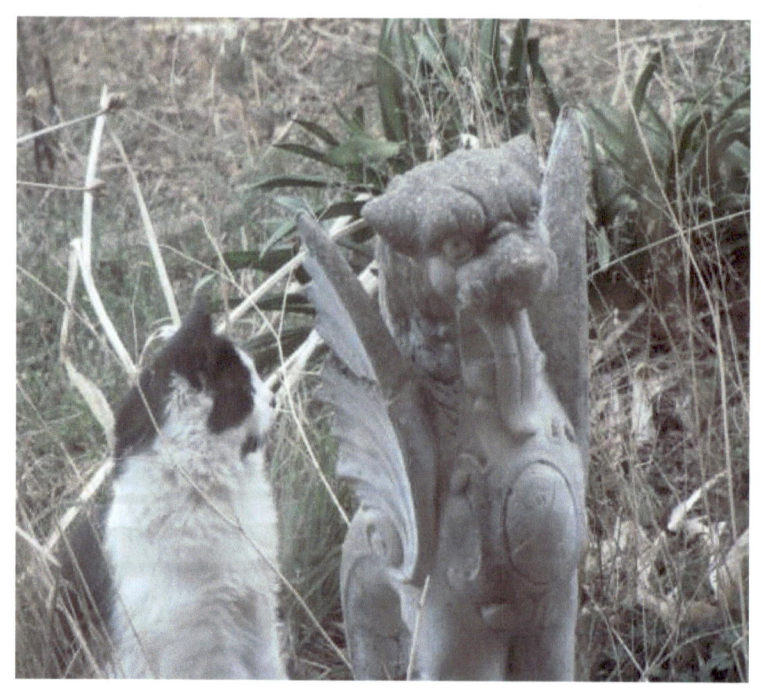

WHAT??

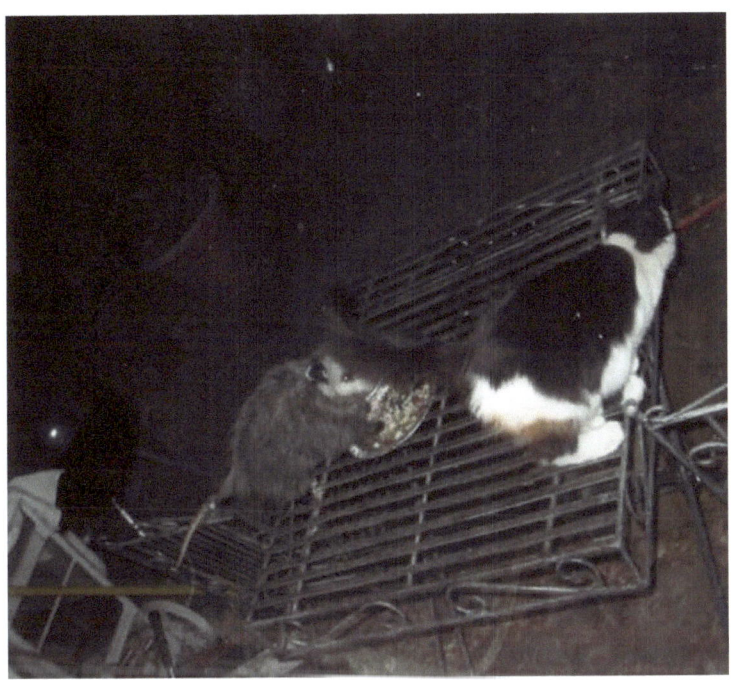

IN YOUR FACE POSSUM, THAT'S MY DINNER!

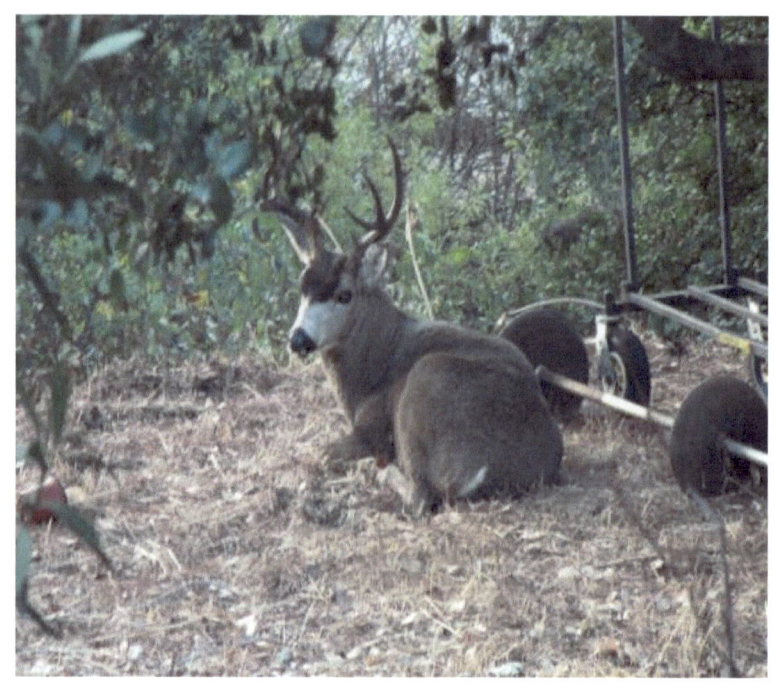

HOW DID I GET IN THIS BOOK?? I ONLY STOPPED BY
FOR A WORKOUT.

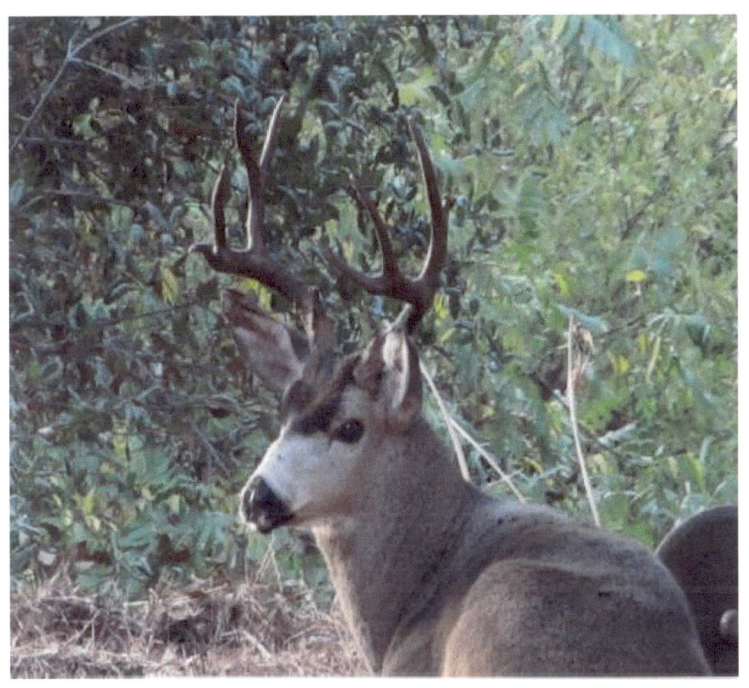

WAS THAT A 10 POINT BUCK WORKING OUT?

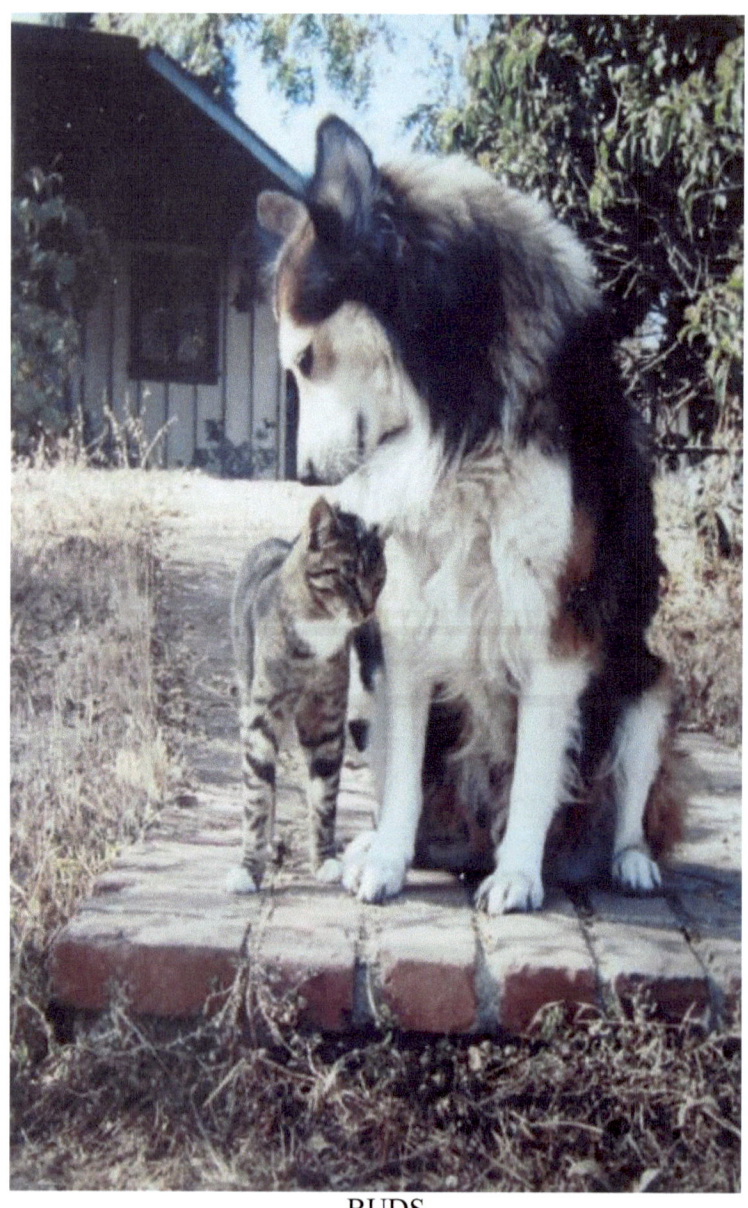

BUDS

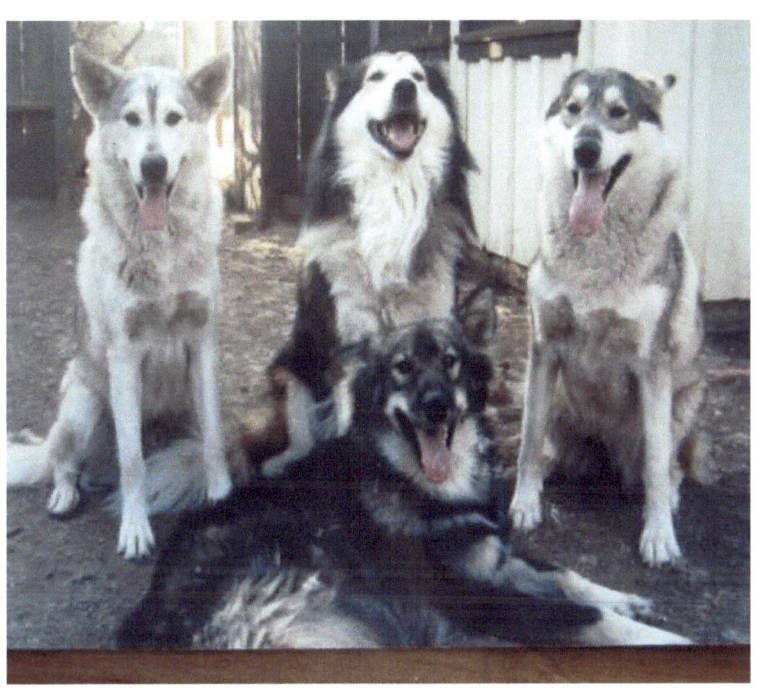

HAVE YOURSELF A MERRY LITTLE CHRISMAS

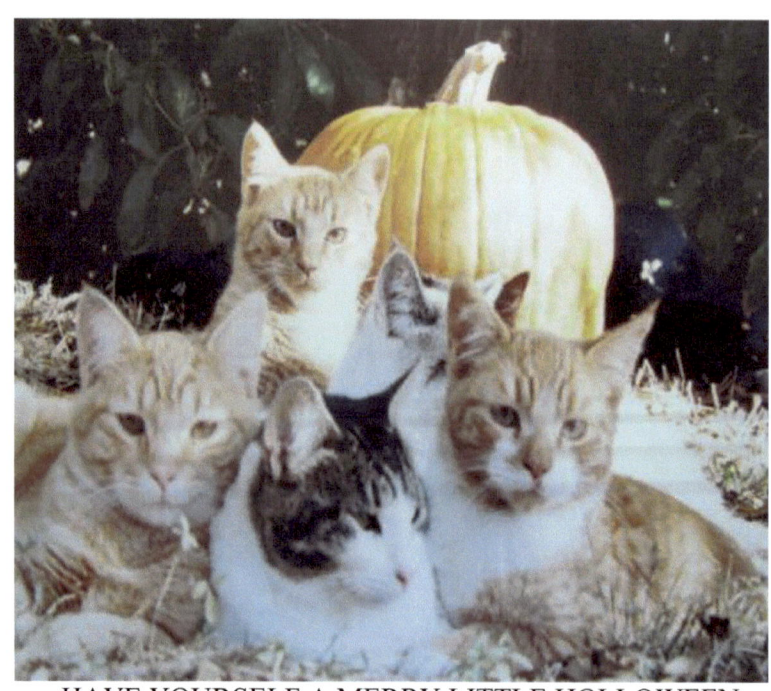

HAVE YOURSELF A MERRY LITTLE HOLLOWEEN

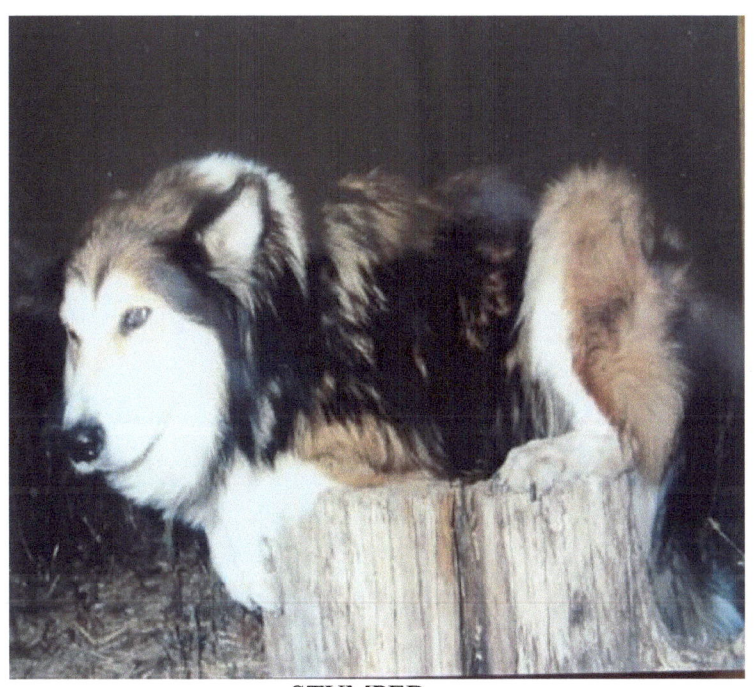

STUMPED

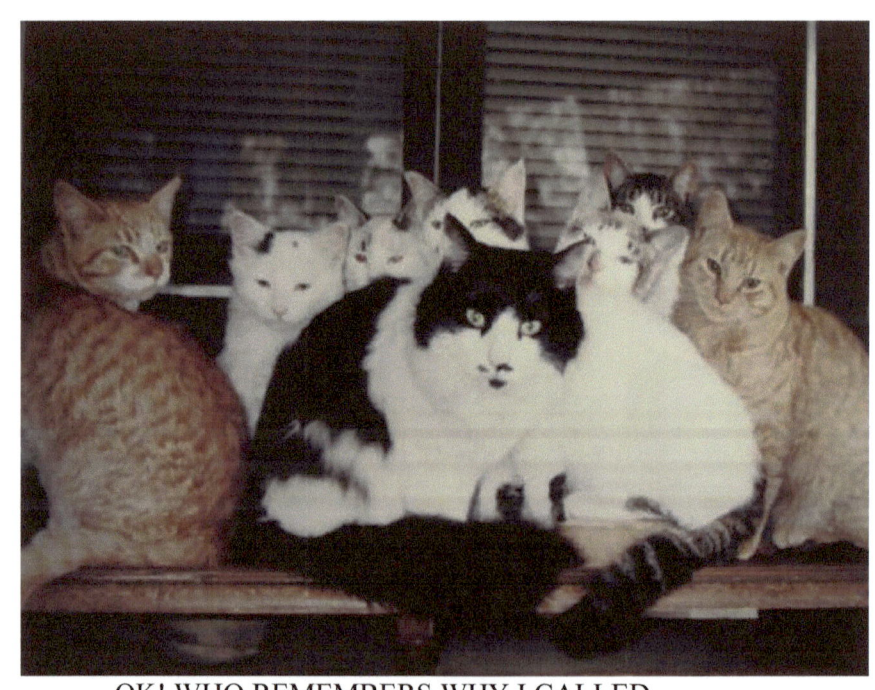

OK! WHO REMEMBERS WHY I CALLED
YOU GUYS TOGETHER?

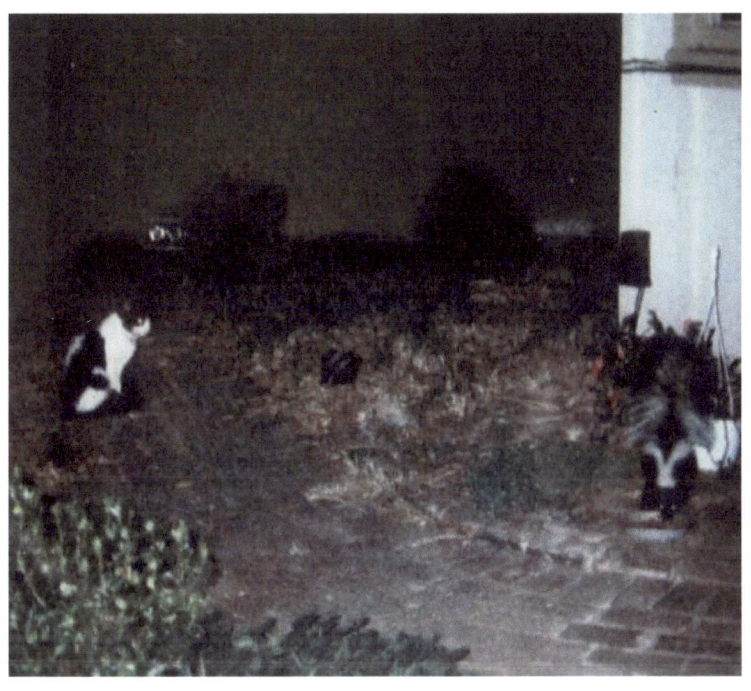

HELLO, ARE YOU MY BLIND DATE?

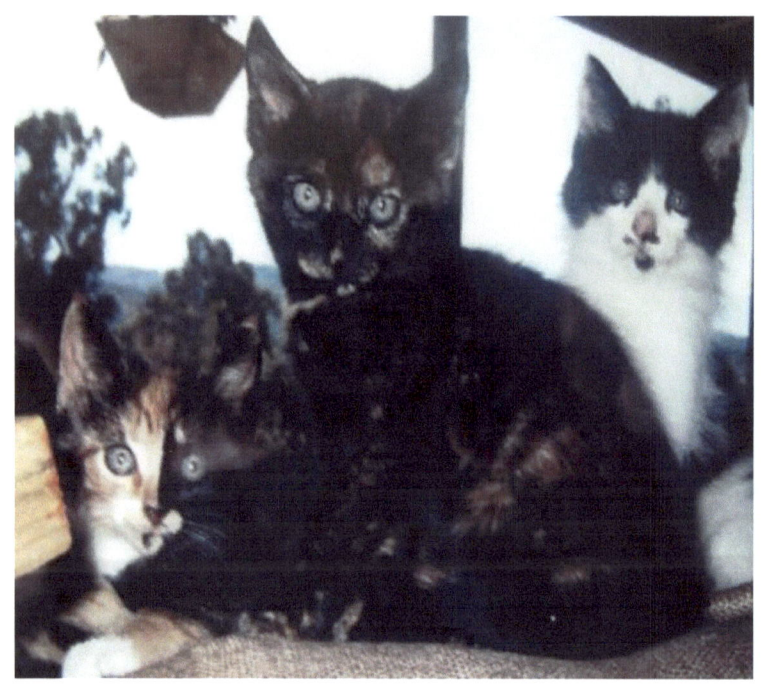

NICE

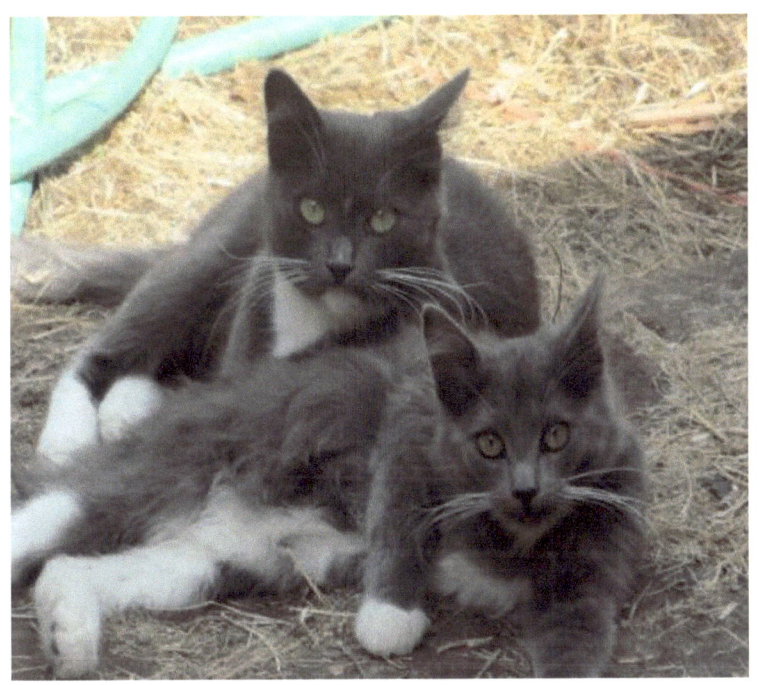

NICE

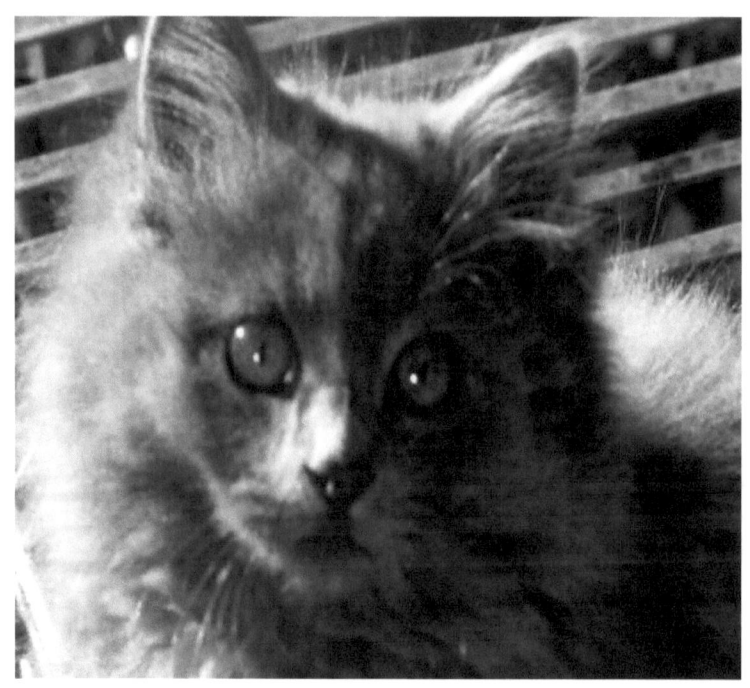

MORE NICE

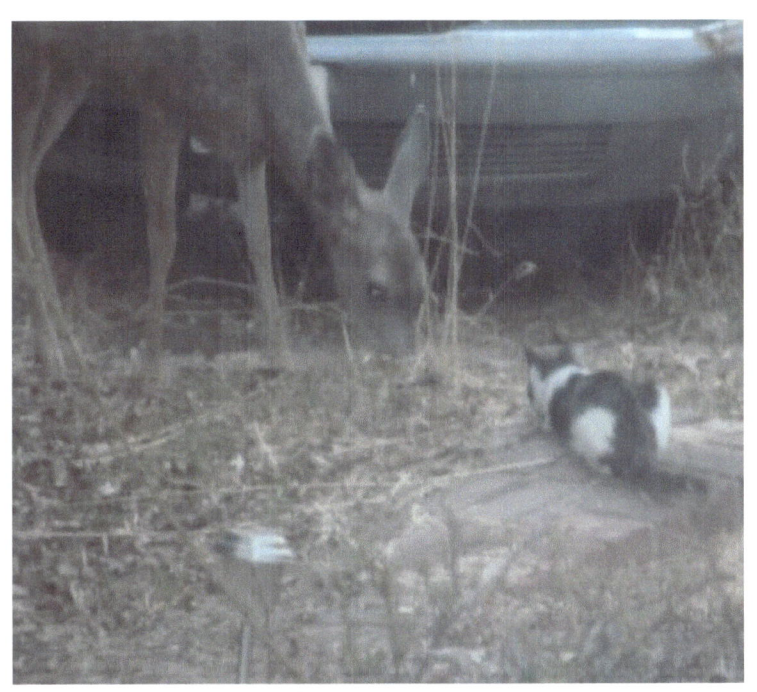

PRE DAWN RENDEZVOUS

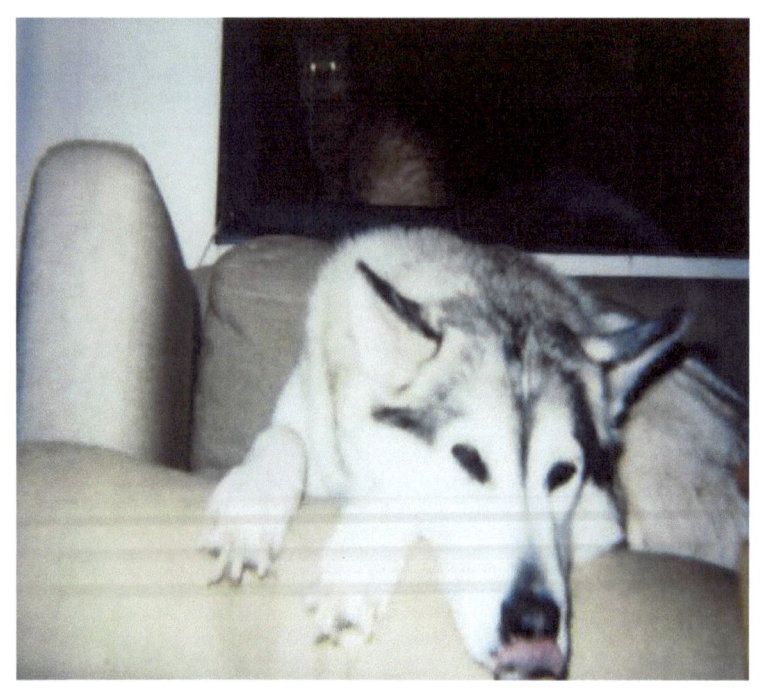

EVER VIGILANT

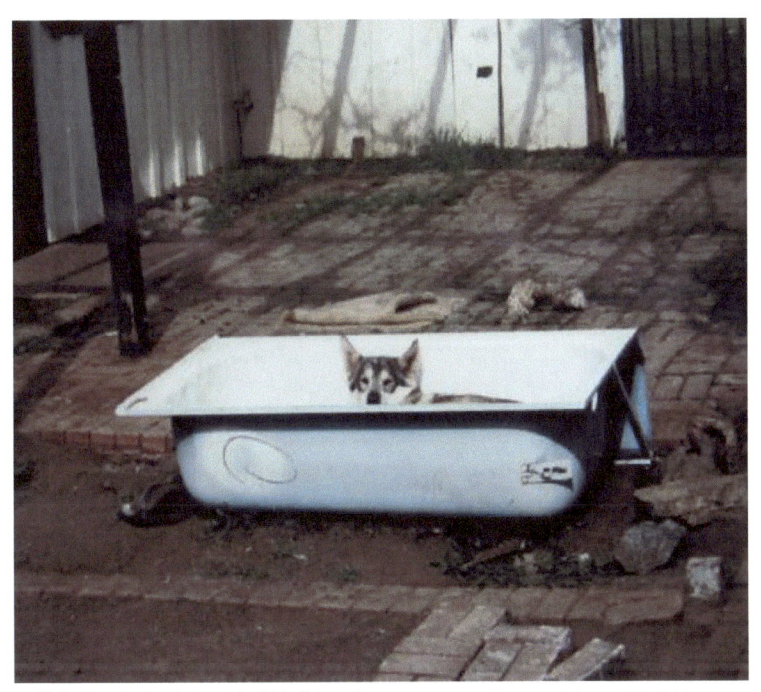

SOLITUDE, CONTEMPLATION, PEACE, AAAAH!

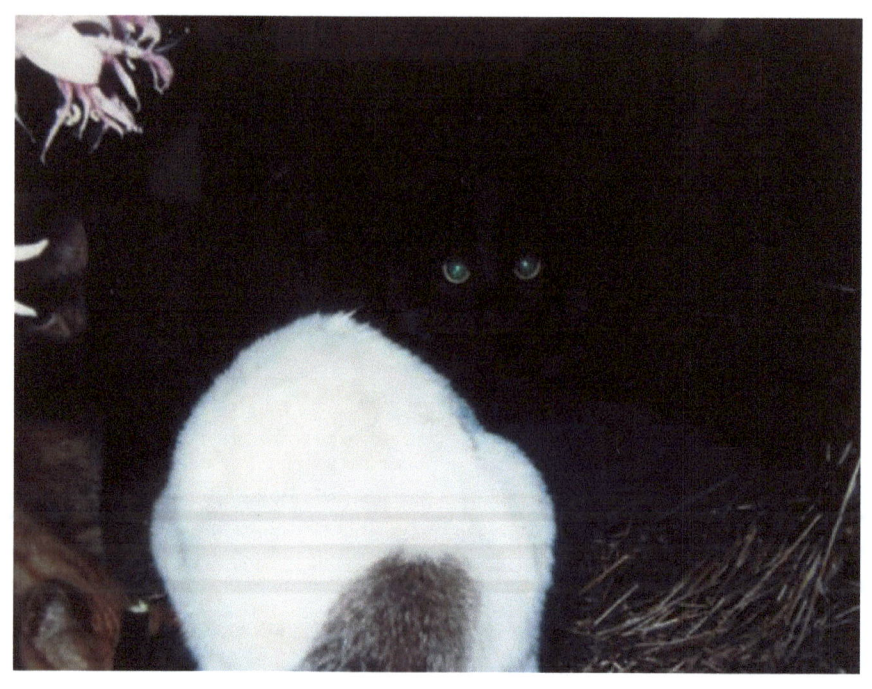

ONE CAT OR TWO??

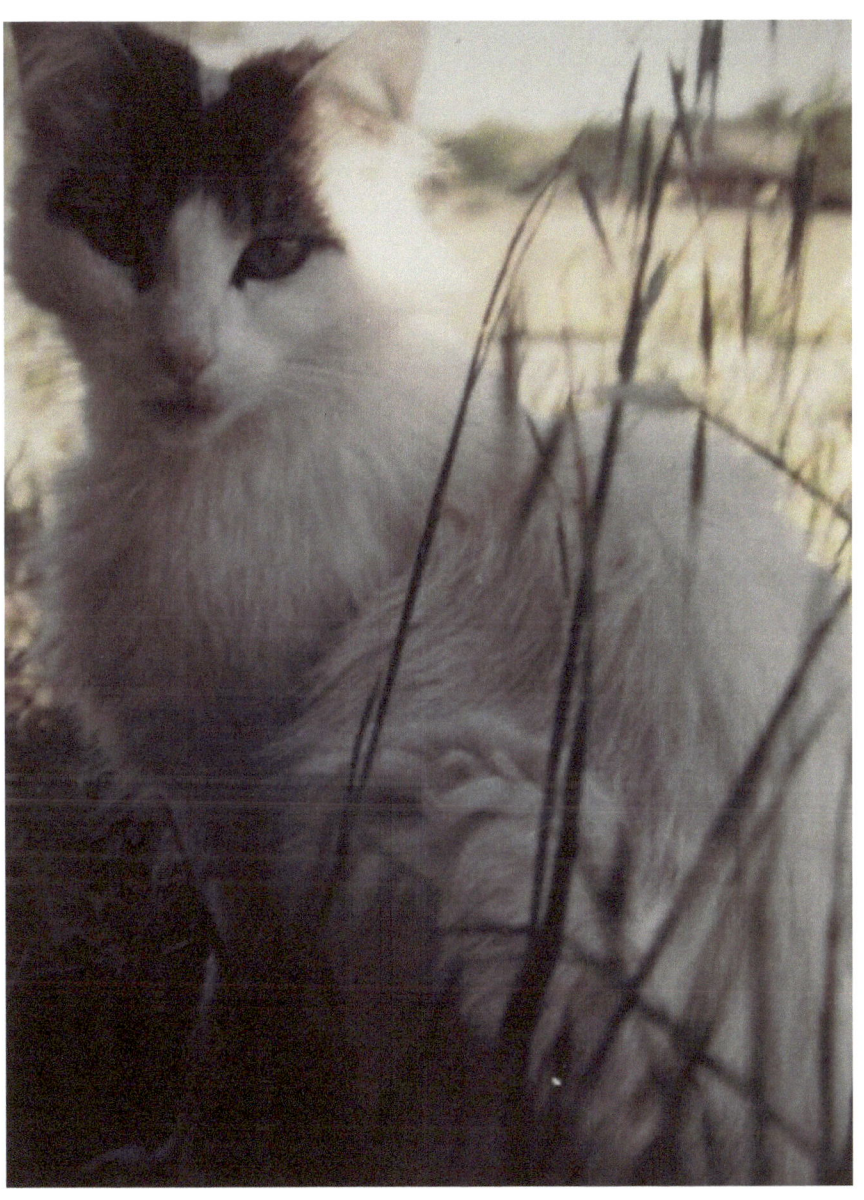

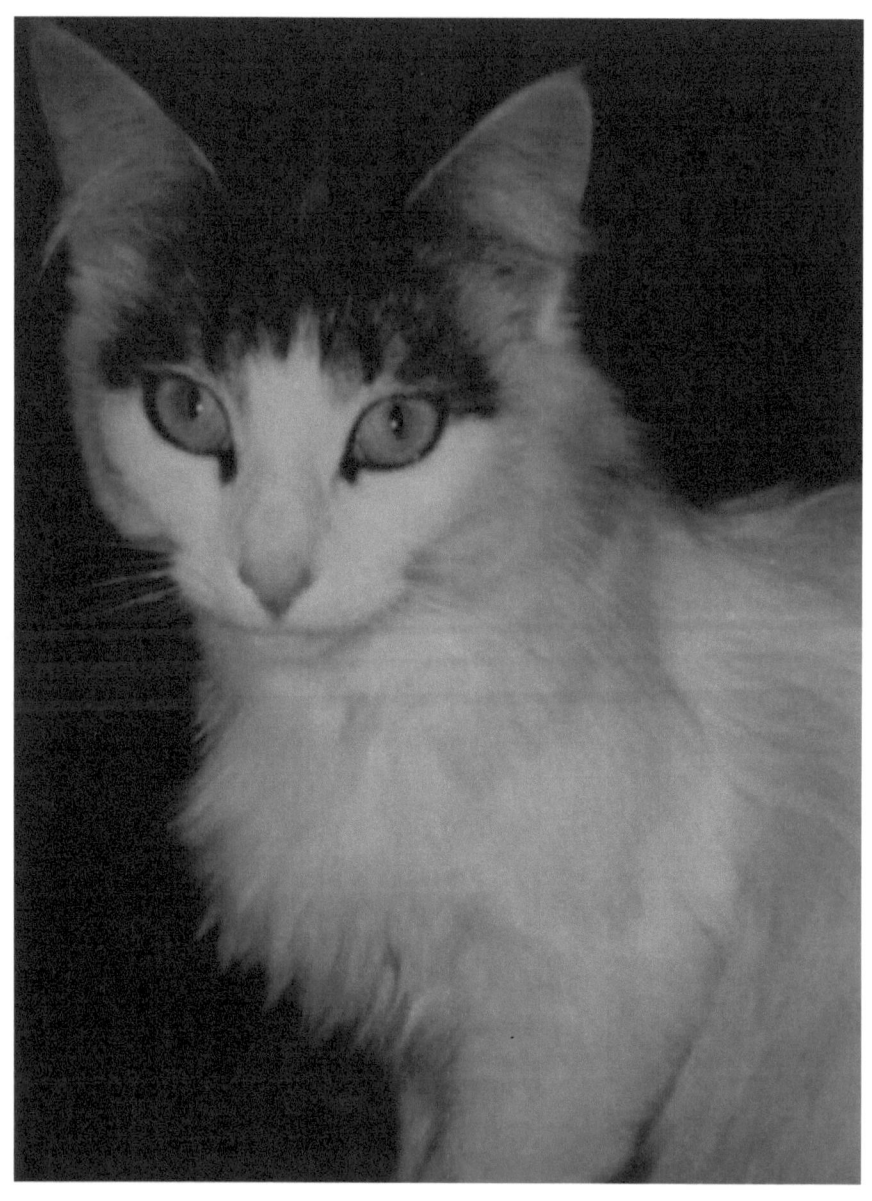

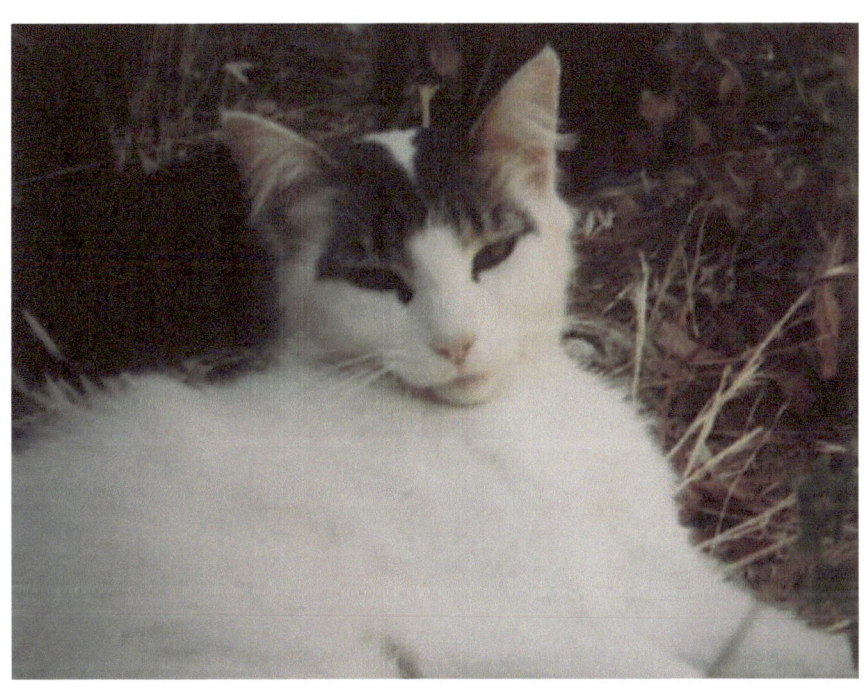

PINKY: FOUNDER OF THE FERAL PRIDE.

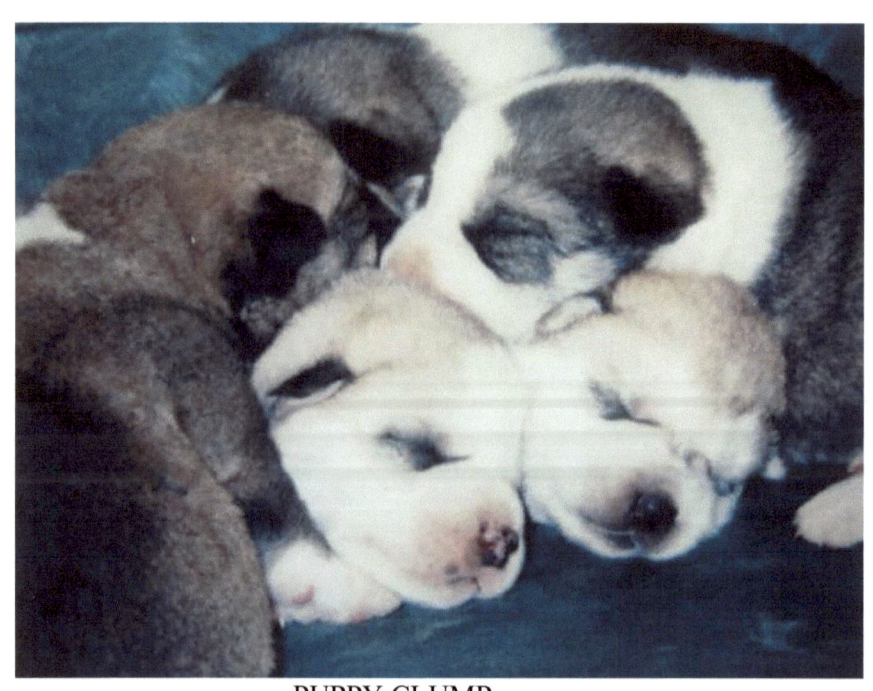

PUPPY CLUMP.

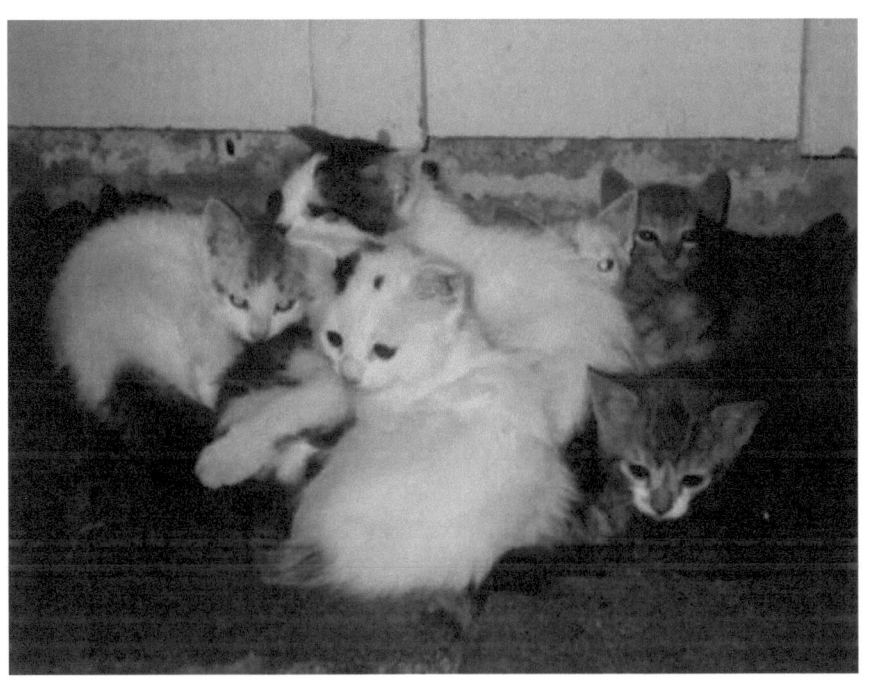

KITTEN CLUMP.

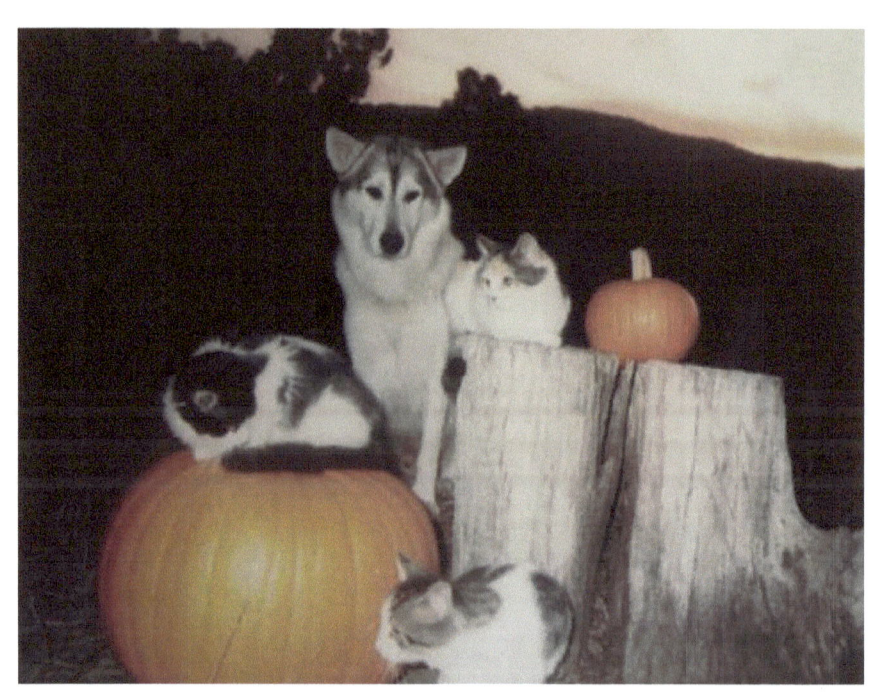

WHO KNOWS HOW TO BAKE
PUMPKIN PIE?

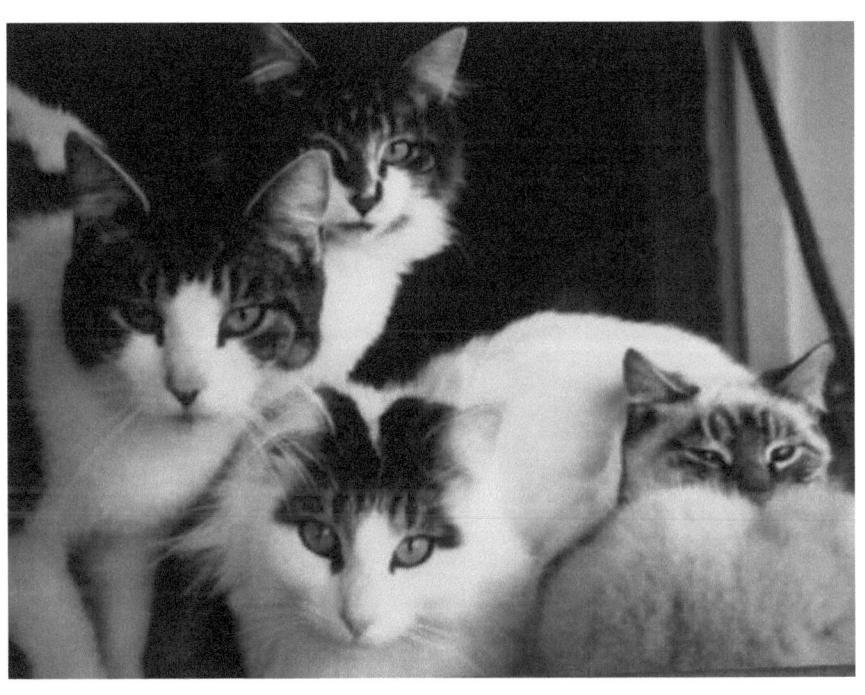

PINKY KEPT HER SISTERS TOGETHER
TO FORM A FERAL PRIDE.

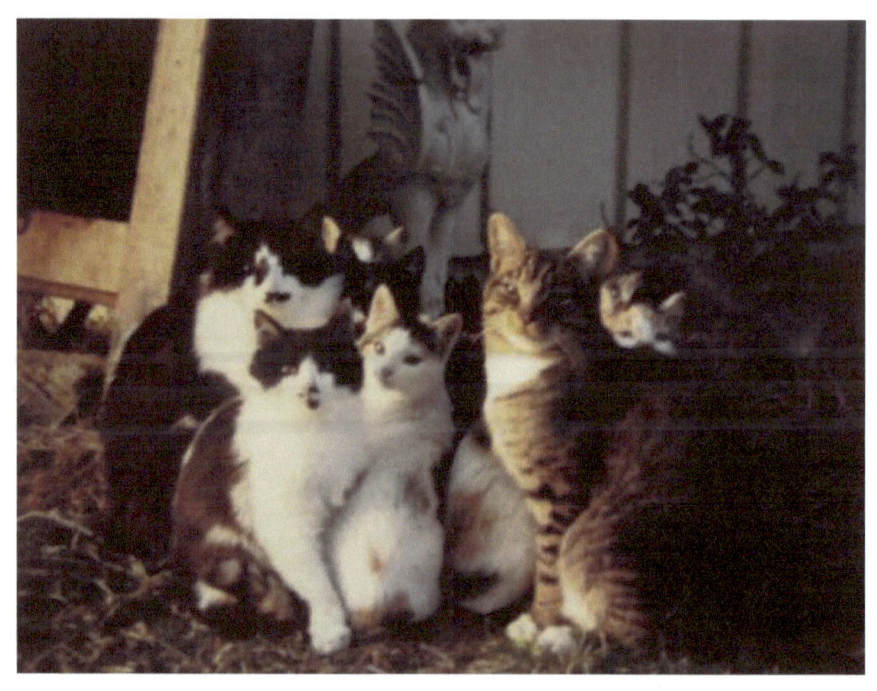

CLUMPING AT FIRST SUN.

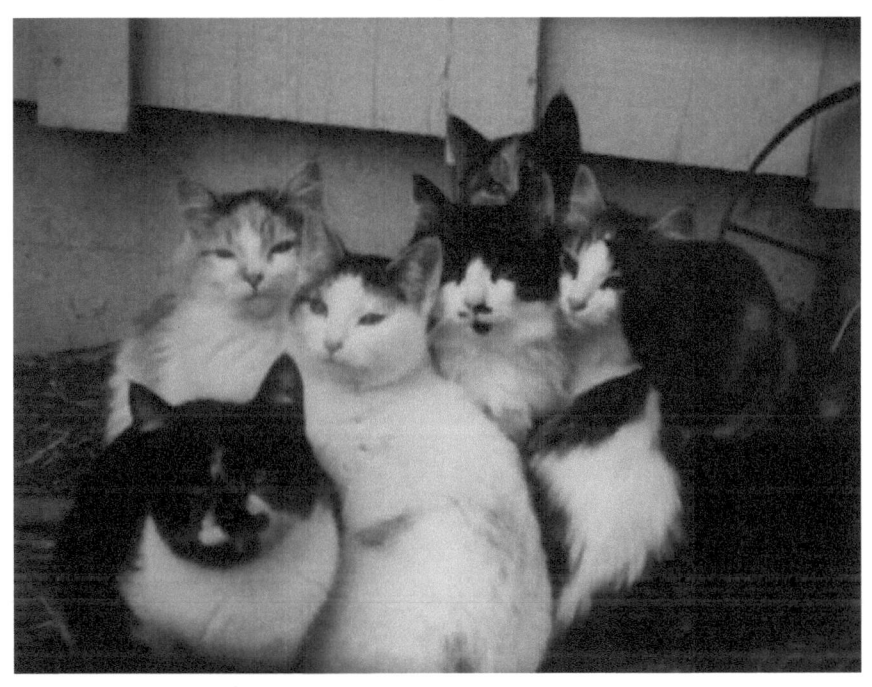

FERAL PRIDE CLUMP.

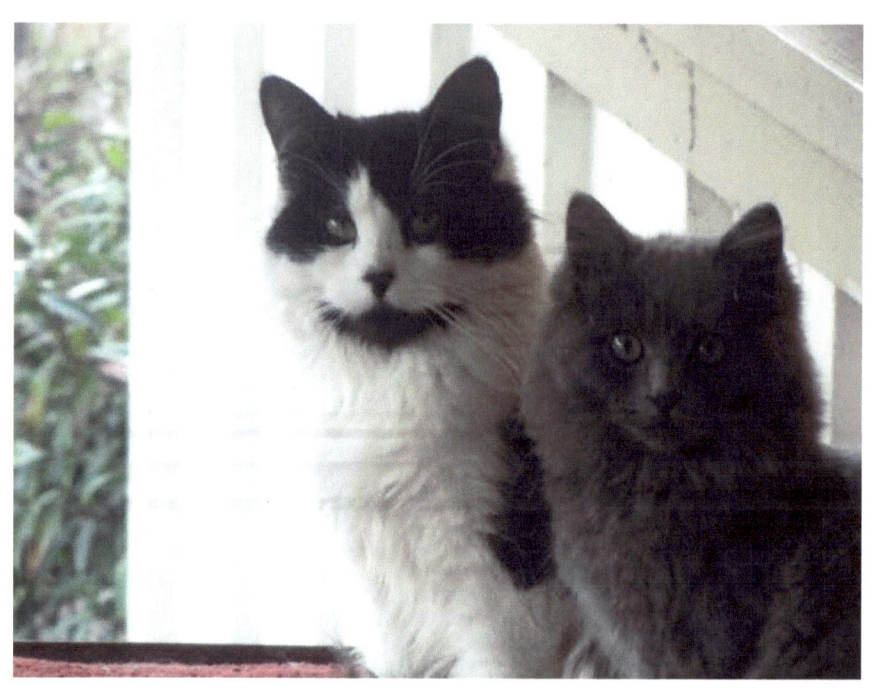

LEANING FERALS.

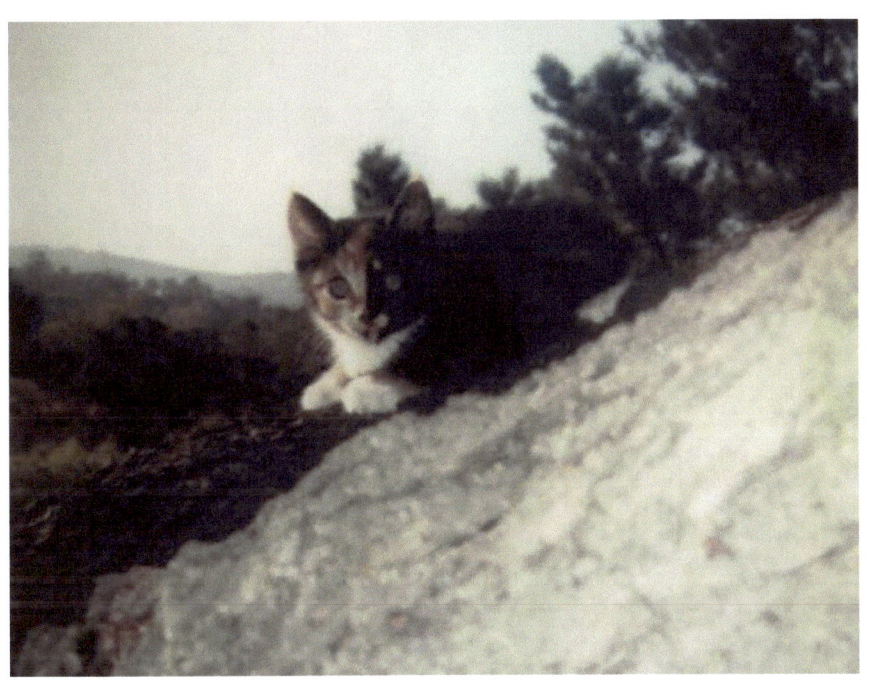

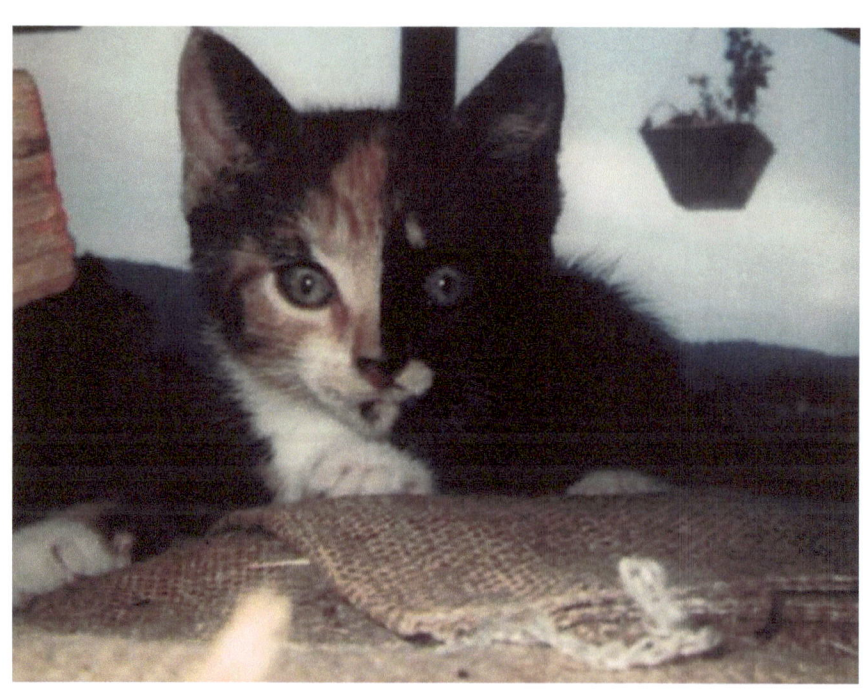

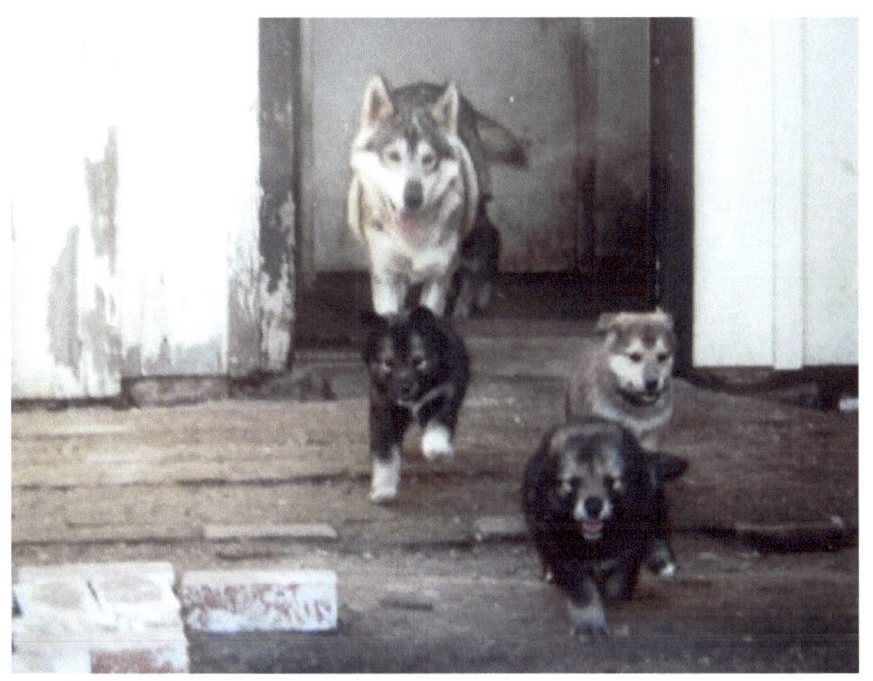

CLASS DISMISSED.

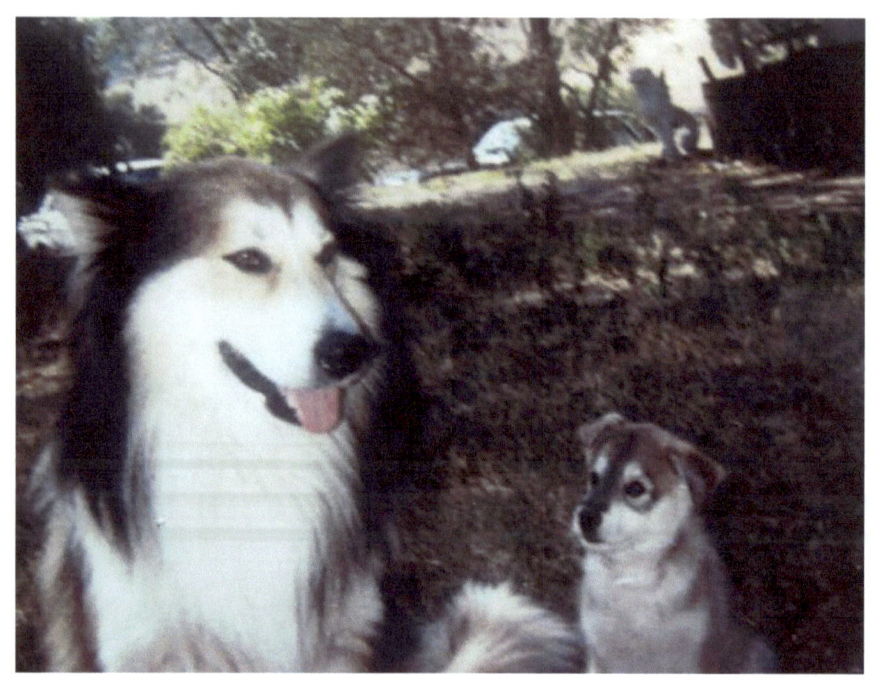

MY DAD.

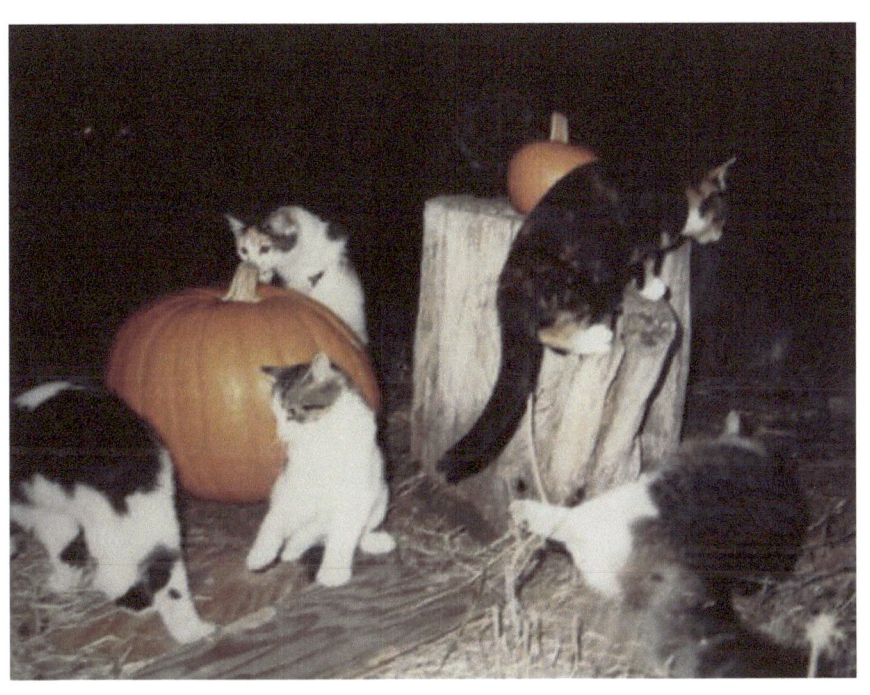

WHAT ARE THESE THINGS?

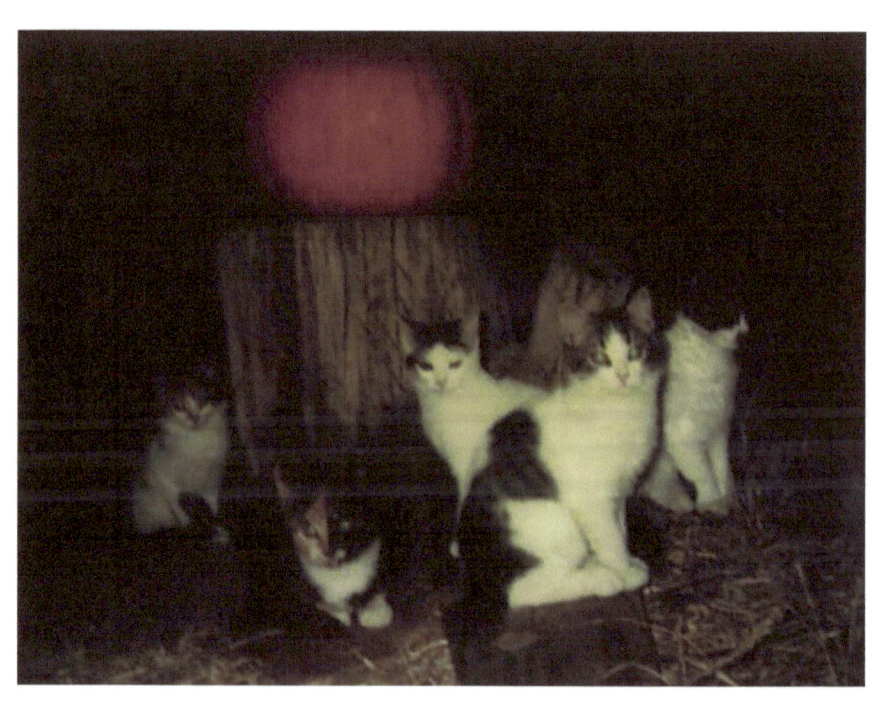

WHATEVER.

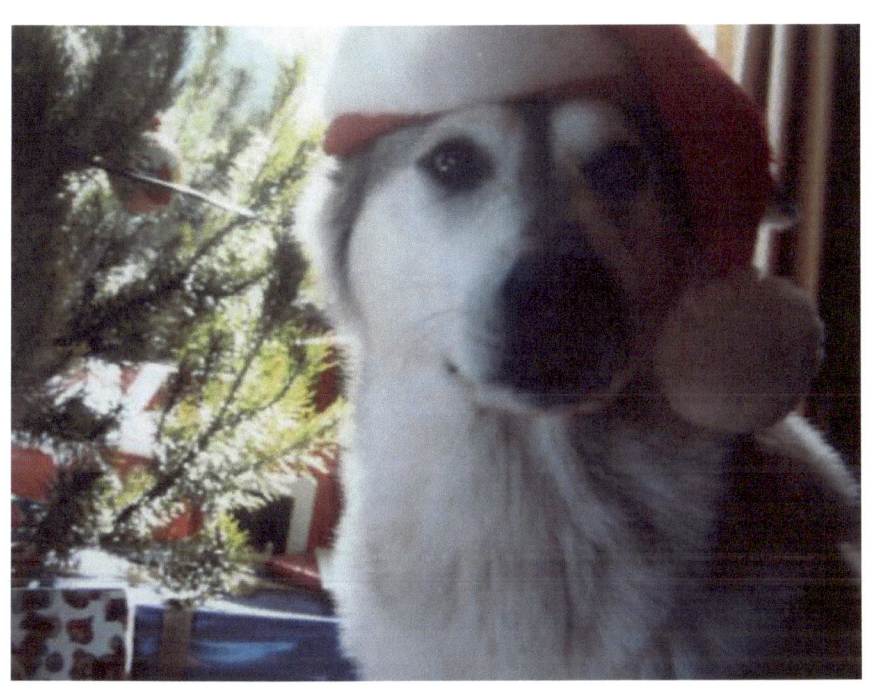

HAPPY HOLIDAYS.

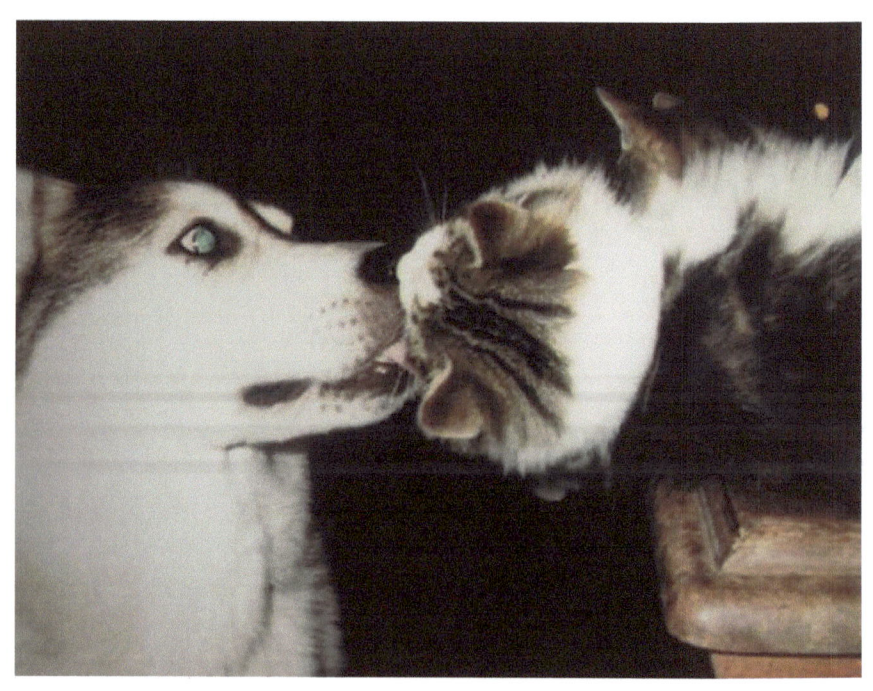

SLEEP SAFE PRINCESS. I'LL KEEP WATCH.
GOOD NIGHT.

www.ingramcontent.com/pod-product-compliance
Lightning Source LLC
Chambersburg PA
CBHW040920180526
45159CB00002BA/544